Leash Training Your Puppy

A Simple and Effective Method for Loose-Leash Walking

By Dale Buchanan

PUPPYTRAINING.DOG

All photos in this book were taken by Dale Buchanan.

ISBN: 9798376937112
Imprint: Independently published

Resources:
- Book Website: http://puppytraining.dog
- Dale's dog training website http://topgundogtraining.com
- Puppy Talk Podcast website http://puppytalkpodcast.com

Introduction

Walking your puppy on a loose leash (no tugging or reacting to stimulus) is one of the most desirable behaviors for every puppy owner. But unfortunately, a tiny percentage of puppy owners ever achieve this goal. The main reasons are improper technique, lack of training, and the wrong equipment.

Leash Training Your Puppy goes way beyond the basics and gets into advanced leash handling techniques that integrate basic dog obedience into the walk to ensure your puppy stays focused on you and under control. Proper leash training requires a commitment to learn the skills and follow through with daily practice.

Walking a puppy calmly on a loose leash is one of the best ways to build a relationship with your puppy. I have found that dogs who can walk great on a loose leash with their owners are usually very obedient and disciplined inside and outside of the house. Dogs that don't pull and react to everything are centered, confident, and calm.

Loose leash walking is a team effort. The owner is the leader, and the puppy is the follower. Don't get this confused with "alpha male" or "dominance." I don't use or suggest that mindset because most of those theories were debunked long ago. Trying to control your puppy through mental or physical force will hurt the puppy's future.

I use positive reinforcement to train puppies using high-value food rewards and a lot of praise. Positive reinforcement training takes time and patience. Follow the guidelines in this book for the best results. The timing of the reinforcement is crucial, and the reward must be something the puppy will love.

"Excellent leash-handling skills are necessary for owners who want their puppy to stop pulling and have excellent leash manners".

Proper Leash Manners

A puppy that walks well on a leash with its owner is usually a puppy that is calm, confident, and well-mannered. You can learn a lot about the relationship between the puppy and its owner by how well they work together while on a walk.

If the puppy is all over the place, on the left side and then the right, picking things up off the ground, and reacting to every other dog, then there is work to be done. But, on the other hand, if you see a puppy that stays next to its owner, is non-reactive to stimuli, and seems relaxed and stress-free, then you know that the owner-puppy relationship is fantastic.

My dog Dixie was about a year old when she finally was great at loose leash walking and not getting super excited at every little thing during our walk. So that's almost 10 months of training, 5-8 walks a day, and practice in the house, with about 2400 practice sessions for loose leash walking in under a year.

It wasn't easy, but the result is a 3-year-old dog with impeccable leash skills. She stays next to me on a loose leash, never pulls, never reacts to any stimulus, and never picks up anything in her mouth off the ground. The best part is that I don't have to give her any commands while on the walk; I stop, and she stops and sits. I move, and she moves. I keep it very simple.

In addition, when I am outside socializing by talking with neighbors while on our walk, Dixie lays down and behaves without any issues. I never tell her anything; she already knows what to do, using her proper leash manners while socializing.

Proper Leash Training Can You Help With:

- Your puppy pulling on the leash.
- Your puppy walking in front of you.
- Your puppy picking things up off the ground.
- Your puppy reacting to stimuli (dogs, people, etc.).
- Your puppy not paying attention to you when there are distractions.
- Your puppy's socialization skills.

When I work with new puppies, I spend a lot of time on leash training because most dogs love to be outside. In addition, the skills taught through loose leash walking transfer into better puppy behaviors inside the house. Of course, this assumes that you have set proper rules and boundaries.

Confidence Building

Puppies need to build confidence to deal with society's stressors. By using simple yet effective desensitization techniques to slowly acclimate your puppy to a variety of new sights and sounds, they become more confident and ready to go for more walks. Failure to do this may result in a fearful or reactive dog later in life.

Notice Dixie's high level of confidence

Leash Training and Puppy Vaccines

Many new puppy owners ask me if they can bring their puppies outside before all of their shots. Unfortunately, this is out of my scope of practice and should be directed to your veterinarian.

If your veterinarian says you should not take your puppy outside, you probably have to listen to them. This is unfortunate, and I may disagree, but you must make the final decision. I can only provide some resources for you to help make that decision. I release all liability for anything that can happen to your puppy in public grass while you're trying to potty train them.

Can You Take Your Puppy Outside before It's Fully Vaccinated?

Yes, it is entirely safe for your puppy to go outside before it is vaccinated, but follow these rules to stay safe. (1) While there is a meager chance of your puppy contracting an illness from playing in the yard or going on a walk, minimize any canine socialization until after his shots are complete. After that, it's okay for your puppy to go in your own yard.

You don't want to socialize your puppy with other dogs that may not be vaccinated or have some unknown disease. You want to wait until your puppy is fully Vaccinated. In other words, you're not taking your puppy to the dog park or doggie daycare.

My puppy, Dixie, got Giardia, a parasite, two times when she was a very young puppy because there was a lot of contaminated feces in the grass of the apartment community where we lived. Our veterinarian gave her some medicine for a few days, and she recovered quickly.

When you start taking your puppy to other areas, you need to know what dog feces or potential diseases are in the grass. This is the problem. It should be fine if you have a yard with a fence, especially a backyard where no other dogs have been.

When Can Puppies Go Outside?

Another element of leash training and taking your puppy outside is socialization. As I've said in many podcast episodes, articles that I've written, and in my book, **The Complete Puppy Training Manual**, the critical period for socializing your puppy will be from 4 to 16 weeks old.

When you get a puppy, you must teach them how to interact with other animals and people in its environment. This will help them understand what safe and appropriate behavior is for them around others. (2)

The critical socialization period ended when the puppy was 16 weeks old. Most new owners receive their puppy at eight weeks old, so you have eight weeks to socialize your puppy. Leash training is a form of socialization; it gets them out of the house.

A puppy shot schedule usually consists of several injections with the same vaccine at 6-8 weeks. After that, the vaccines are repeated every few weeks until your puppy is 16 weeks old.

To protect your new puppy against dangerous diseases, you need to take the following precautions for a puppy that is younger than 16 weeks old:

- First, get your puppy all his vaccines as recommended by the veterinarian.

- Do not take your puppy to places other dogs tend to frequent, like a pet store or dog park.

- Make sure to carry your puppy in and out of a vet's office or hospital. Veterinary staff will take every precaution to protect puppies from infectious diseases. Still, a sick dog may contaminate a rest area, the floor, or furniture before the veterinary staff can disinfect it. So, be safe and make sure to carry your puppy.

- Do not let your puppy interact with animal feces as they are walking; don't let them interact with other dogs if you aren't aware of their vaccination history.

- Always ensure that the other dogs in your home are current on their vaccines.

- Only let your puppy access a fenced yard. If your neighbor has a dog, let them know your pup has yet to be completely vaccinated.

An Alternative Option

I strongly advise gaining using pee pads in the house. If you are adamant about following the rules of your veterinarian, and they say, "Absolutely no way that your dog's going in any grass until they've had all of their vaccines," here is one final option. It's called Fresh Patch®. It's actual green grass

What About Corrections?

Some mild corrections for young puppies are OK. This is why we teach the leave-it command and use the sound "uh-uh" to prevent the puppy from picking things up in their mouth on walks.

Firm corrections and yelling at your puppy could easily cause some fear and anxiety in the puppy and hurt your relationship with them. Therefore, be careful how many corrections you use and your intention behind them.

PRO TIP: Remember that these are suggestions without guaranteeing the outcome. If you cannot achieve the desired results from the advice in this book, it's best to consult or hire a dog trainer in your area who can help you.

Leash Training Equipment

You will need a variety of leashes. You will want a six-foot snap leash, a flat collar, a front clip harness, a rear clip harness, and a long line (a 15' or 30' leash). Do not get a retractable leash. They cause problems I will address in the chapter on Leash Training.

One dog harness I recommend is the Easy Walk® Harness by PetSafe®. This harness has a clip on the front with a patented martingale loop that prevents the puppy from pulling. It's easy to get on and off the puppy and built to last. I do not recommend a rear clip harnesses for leash training because they teach your puppy to pull. However, the back clip harness will be used for enrichment walks, which we will discuss in more detail in the chapter on The Loose Leash Technique.

Another dog harness I recommend is the Freedom No-Pull Harness by 2 Hounds Design. This harness has a front and back clip. The back clip can be used for enrichment walks. Use the front and back clips together to control pulling and redirect your dog's attention for training walks. Again, the same manufacturer sells the proper leashes that work with this harness.

Equipment for Puppies Ages 8 weeks to 6 Months:

- Easy Walk® Harness
- Freedom Harness by 2 Hounds Design
- 6-foot leash
- Long lead = 15, 20, or 30-foot leash
- Flat collar

I do not recommend a retractable leash, shown below, because they teach your puppy to pull and can be cumbersome. In addition, they can also be dangerous because of the poor quality material used for the leash itself.

**I DO NOT SUGGEST A
RETRACTABLE LEASH**

Why I Recommend a Front Clip Harness

The Easy Walk® Harness by PetSafe has a patented design of the front clip mechanism with a Martingale loop that prevents pulling. A rear clip harness does not achieve this result. Therefore, I like this harness for leash training and loose leash walking.

I have demonstrated many times with my clients who use a rear clip harnesses how the Easy Walk® Harness relaxes the puppy and helps teach them to walk better on a loose leash. Pulling, lunging, and jumping immediately stops, and the puppy owner can enjoy the walks.

The Freedom Harness by 2 Hounds Design has both a front and rear clip. This harness requires a unique leash to use both. This harness is excellent for leash training, loose leash walking, and enrichment walks.

Both of these harnesses are highly recommended by dog trainers around the world because they work.

Three Types of Walks

I use three types of walks for puppies that I train. Each of these walks is unique and can be combined to achieve multiple goals in one outing. Roughly 40% of your walks will be potty breaks, 40% will be training walks (loose leash walking), and 20% will be enrichment walks. Your puppy needs to have a balance of all three to develop obedience, discipline, and social skills necessary for adulthood.

1) The Training Walk

During this walk, you will add some basic obedience directly into the walk. For example, you take 20 steps, stop, and ask your puppy to sit. Have them wait 10 seconds to learn patience, and then start again. Do this consistently for a few weeks each walk, and then add the down command after the sit. Again, have your puppy wait patiently, and then continue the walk. For this walk, you will need a front clip harness with a 6-foot leash or a flat collar with a 6-foot leash.

In the chapter Leash Training Drills, I will discuss more about the training walk and some fun exercises you can do with your puppy.

2) The Enrichment Walk

You will need a rear clip harness and a long line for this walk. A long line is a 15-30 foot leash, not a retractable leash, allowing the puppy to forage and roll around in the grass, smell some bushes, and have fun. There is no obedience training in this walk; that will defeat the point. You allow the puppy to begin making decisions outside instead of being constantly told what to do. The only time you would give commands is for the puppy's safety, for example, if they are picking up something terrible in their mouth.

**Dixie playing in the grass during
an Enrichment Walk**

I DO NOT recommend a retractable leash for the enrichment walk, because it can be unsafe and cumbersome. They also teach your puppy to pull, which is the opposite of what we want with loose leash walking.

3) The Potty Break Walk

This is a simple walk to have your puppy potty outside in the grass. You can use a flat collar or any harness for the potty break. For more information on potty training, please read my other book *Potty Training Your Puppy*.

Incorporating All Three Walks

If you have time, you can incorporate 2-3 of these types of walks together. For example, you can take your puppy out for a potty break and add a few minutes of loose leash walking combined with obedience. First, have your puppy sit and wait to learn patience. Then, give the down command, and teach them to do that with distractions. Every chance you get to add some loose leash walking and obedience into the walk, even if it's a potty break, you should do it.

NOTE: You can see these leash training demonstrations on this YouTube channel: https://www.youtube.com/c/TopGunDogTraining; go to the playlist Leash Training.

The long line is great for playing fetch when you don't have a fenced in yard

When using two hands, you want to place your thumb through the loop at the end of the leash and lightly grab the middle of the leash with your other hand. You can choke up on the leash, as needed, to shorten the puppy's distance from you. Move your hand down the leash, as shown in the photos below, to bring your puppy closer to you. Give your puppy more freedom by sliding your hand up the leash.

How To Hold The Leash - Two Handed Method

PRO TIP: If you have arthritis and cannot use your fingers as described above, do the best you can with your entire hand but try not to put too much pressure on the leash with your hand. In addition, thicker leashes with diameters between 1/2" and 1" thick may help if you have arthritis. These are generally easy to grab.

Body Posture

The posture of your body and the way position your arm is very important. Your body, shoulder, arm, wrist, and fingers should be relaxed. Any tension will be transmitted through the leash to your puppy.

Keep your head up and forward, creating a vision of where you are going and scanning the area for any potential threats, such as off-leash dogs, cars, etc.

Loose Leash Walking Step 1

Practice this step in your home. After putting your leash, harness, or collar on your puppy, let them be calm and do nothing. Don't give any commands, don't take a step. Allow your puppy to get acclimated to the leash and be guided by you. Once your puppy sits on their own without any commands, mark and reward that behavior. Open the front door, and give the command "stay" while they are in the sit position. Remember only to provide the command once, do not repeat commands. Make the puppy wait with the front door open, sitting patiently for the next step. Don't go on any walks until you have completed this step.

Loose Leash Walking Step 2

Once you have completed Step 1, you're ready to bring your puppy outside. I suggest only going to the driveway if you live in a house or on the sidewalk in an apartment or condo. Avoid the grass for now unless this is a potty break, and the puppy is ready to eliminate. Get that over quickly, and return to the hard surface for training. Use the same technique in step 1, allowing your puppy to figure out they need to sit and do nothing. Once they do, mark and reward that behavior. The puppy needs to learn to relax and accept your leadership before going on the walk.

Loose Leash Walking Step 3

Take a few steps with your puppy without them pulling on the leash or walking in front of you. If they try to pull or walk too fast, stop walking and allow them to go back into the sit position. Slowing them down physically will slow down their brain from overthinking and being reactive. Try to walk a short distance of 2-3 feet with a loose leash. Don't expect to walk more than a few steps at a time before having to stop.

Loose Leash Walking Step 4

Now, try walking a little further. If your puppy begins to pull, change directions 180 degrees with a U-turn. This will confuse the puppy and get them to stop overthinking and trying to figure things out. They need to learn to work as a team and follow your lead. Doing U-turns is very effective and best done when they are not on the grass because it's too distractive. I like using the driveway, street, or parking lot.

PRO TIP:
If your puppy starts to pull, and you pull back in a linear motion, you will reinforce the pulling. Instead, create circles by

redirecting your puppy from the side, having them move in a circular motion and back to loose leash walking. See the images below.

| Puppy pulling | Redirecting from the side, not pulling straight back | Notice the loose leash, as puppy comes back to me |

Loose Leash Walking Step 5

Start going for the training walk with slightly longer distances and no distractions. Remember that each time your puppy pulls or reacts to anything, they are rehearsing that behavior, and it's being automatically reinforced. The goal in this step is to go 20-30 feet and stop, allowing the puppy to sit and wait. Mark the behavior with a "yes" and give a food reward. No commands are needed except for one "sit." DO NOT repeat commands or show too much affection in the form of praise because this will only overstimulate and excite the puppy. You're trying to keep them focused on the training.

Loose Leash Walking Step 6

Start taking your puppy for longer walks, with minor distractions such as cars driving by, people walking by, and other dogs walking with their owners from a distance. Puppies must slowly be desensitized to all the stimuli that cause them

turns for 10 repetitions to provide enough time for them to focus and obey the owners.

NOTE: The u-turn is also helpful for reactive puppies, with more details in the Managing Leash Reactivity chapter.

Stop! Back-Up

This is an excellent drill for your puppy to learn how to focus and follow you. I like to use this also as part of the recall, come command, and when the puppy is distracted. You can do this drill on the sidewalk.

While on your walk, and your puppy is slightly out in front of you, stop and begin walking backward quickly. Say your puppy's name and the command "come." When the puppy turns around, focuses on you, and begins moving toward you, say "good boy" or "good girl." Once they get to you, place them in a sit, mark the behavior, and give them a food reward.

Left Turns

\With your puppy on your right side, you will walk them as usual and do a sharp 90-degree left turn. Your puppy will be outside the turn, as in the diagram below. Do three more to form a complete square and arrive at your starting position. Stop and give your puppy the "sit" command. Make them wait patiently to start the same drill again, four 90-degree repetitions, for a full 360 degrees. Repeat this drill for 5 sets.

NOTE: The left turn with your puppy on your right is much easier than the right turn you will do next.

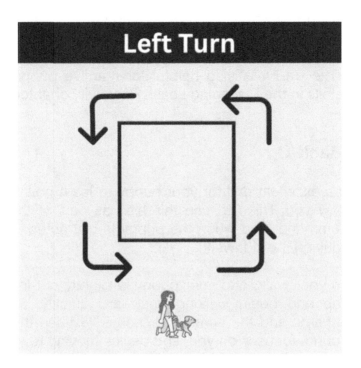

Left Turn

Right Turns

With your puppy on your right side, you will walk them as usual and do a sharp 90-degree right turn. Your puppy will be inside the turn, as in the diagram below. Do three more to form a complete square and arrive at your starting position. Stop and give your puppy the "sit" command. Make them wait patiently to start the same drill again, four 90-degree repetitions, for a full 360 degrees. Repeat this drill for 5 sets.

You will have to use some leash manipulation during this drill because you will be cutting in front of your puppy with each 90-degree turn, and they MUST stay next to you at all times for this to work effectively. Keep them from falling behind or getting in front of you because this drill will not work effectively if they do.

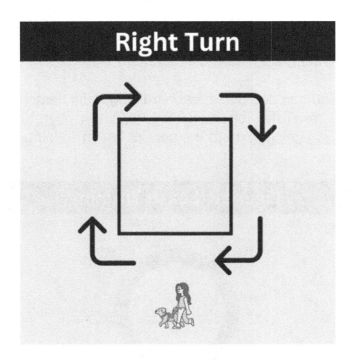

The Figure 8

The Figure 8 is the best way to teach your puppy to stay next to you on a loose leash. This drill keeps your puppy focused on you at all times instead of getting distracted.

This drill combines the left and right turns, creating circles instead of squares. You will be doing some circles with your puppy on the outside of you and some with your puppy on the inside without stopping.

Don't allow your puppy to pick stuff up off of the ground or react to anything during the Figure 8. This is a training session. Later, you can take your puppy on an enrichment walk (as described in another chapter). You can allow your puppy more freedom to have fun during the enrichment walk.

This may include playing in the grass, chasing a butterfly, and running around. As long as they stay out of trouble, pretty much anything goes for the enrichment walk.

NOTE: You can see these leash training drills demonstrations on this YouTube channel: https://www.youtube.com/c/TopGunDogTraining; go to the playlist Leash Training.

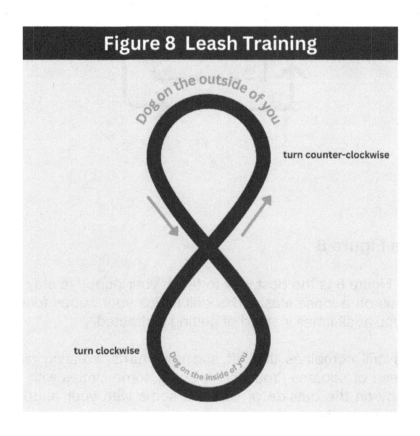

Figure 8 Leash Training

Dog on the outside of you

turn counter-clockwise

turn clockwise

Dog on the inside of you

addition, your dog walker is NOT a dog trainer. They are only there to help you manage the puppy and take it out for a potty break and enrichment walk, not a training walk. Most dog walkers cannot correct your puppy or know what to do if they pull on the leash. That's not their job.

The Heel Position

I will explain briefly how to teach your dog the heel position, which is the heel of your foot in line with the dog's front foot. I do not recommend using the heel command or position when teaching a young puppy to walk on a loose leash. It's too restrictive and unnecessary. The heel command ensures that your puppy stays directly beside you while walking, and young puppies just starting are not likely to comply without resistance.

The heel position is great for K9 dogs trained off-leash or in obedience competitions, so the dog stays next to the handler, but it's not needed for the average house dog walking around your neighborhood. We encourage the puppy to have space between us; at the same time, we don't want them pulling a lot and reacting to every little stimulus.

The heel command is also one of the most misused and misunderstood commands in puppy training. I have seen people walking their puppies demanding the heel position by repeating the command "heel" loudly and firmly, and the puppy does absolutely nothing. Doing this can overstimulate the puppy and hurt the owner-puppy relationship.

Training The Heal Position

If you want to teach the heal position, you will need high-value food rewards. I prefer chicken breast or beef liver treats. Also, you want something larger than training treads because you will be holding the food in your hand next to your side while you walk your puppy. You can see a video of a client doing this on my Youtube channel Top Gun Dog Training, under the Leash Training playlist.

With your hand slightly open, holding the food for your puppy to smell, keep your hand dropped down to the side of your leg. Allow the puppy to smell the food but do not let them have it. Start walking, and your puppy should follow you by your side, with their nose near your hand. Take a short walk, stop, and raise your hand, forming a 90-degree angle at your elbow. The puppy should sit next to your leg with the heel of your foot in line with the puppy's front foot. This means you are slightly ahead of your puppy by a few inches.

This is the heal position. Anything more than this simple instruction would require advanced training and months of practice. As I mentioned already, young puppies, full of energy and curiosity, are unlikely to walk or sit in the heel position. It can be very restrictive and cause more stress in the puppy than they already have. Remember, The goal is to eliminate stress and help the puppy relax.

The Heel Position

Building Leadership

Think about the great leaders of our time and what qualities they possess—confidence, calmness, good communication skills, discipline, structure, and mindfulness. You can use these qualities when raising your puppy. Failure to be this type of leader for your puppy means they may not learn properly and could develop serious behavior issues as an adult dog.

My relationship with my dog Dixie, whom I have had for 2 years, is fantastic. I have used these leadership skills to raise her since she was ten weeks old. I showed her the way, and she's easily the most obedient, social, and calm dog most people will ever meet.

My last dog Spaulding was a Lab Mix that I rescued in May 2008. Our relationship was solid as a rock and apparent when we were in public together. I took him everywhere, and he was always calm, balanced, and obedient. He never had any behavior problems and was very easy to live with. Unfortunately, he passed in April 2020, and I still miss him and think about him a lot.

Leadership is a skill that has to be learned. You understand leadership if you have owned a company and successfully managed people. If you have raised kids, then you have the qualities. Anyone in the military clearly understands leadership. Learn to tap into those skills and use them to raise your puppy.

I learned leadership skills by studying martial arts starting when I was 19. I took lessons from a Korean Grand Master in Tae Kwon Do for ten years, who taught his students how to defend themselves and become great leaders. I use these leadership skills to train dogs and raise my own. If you have

THRESHOLD

Under	At	Above
Under Threshold The puppy shows no signs of reactivity to the stimulus present.	**At Threshold** The point at which the puppy goes from showing no reactivity to showing some reactivity.	**Above Threshold** The puppy shows apparent signs of reactivity to the stimulus present.

The reactivity can be a combination of fear, anxiety, excitement, or hyperactivity

The stimulus can be another dog, person, car, or any combination of sights or sounds that make your puppy react.

A recommended method to eliminate the stimuli is to take walks when no stimuli are present. Time your walks around the triggers until the reactivity has been improved by yourself or a professional dog trainer.

When working with reactive puppies, the second tip is to teach an incompatible behavior that will take the place of reactivity. For example, if your puppy starts to pull towards another dog when they see it, teach them to stop, sit, and watch you instead.

Working with reactive puppies and dogs takes a lot of time, and the outcome can vary from one puppy to another. When trying to understand why a puppy reacts, there are many variables, such as age, socialization level, breed, size, and medical history. Puppies that were not socialized early on in their life, from 4-12 weeks old, are more likely to develop reactivity while walking outside on a leash.

Be patient, and set your expectations appropriately. Nothing is worse than trying to rush a puppy into being something that it may not be capable of doing right away. Training a reactive puppy or dog takes time, energy, and dedication.

There are three things you need to do to manage a reactive puppy. Remember that this will not necessarily change the puppy's behavior. However, it can help manage the situation and prevent your puppy from rehearsing the reactivity.

1. Creating Distance BEFORE the reactivity occurs.
2. Train Within the Puppies Threshold.
3. Stay Out of the Red Zone.

Here are two more techniques I can recommend to help manage reactive puppies.

U-Turns

As described in the chapter Leash Training Drills, U-Turns are a great way to get your puppy out of a troublesome situation. If you have a reactive puppy, you need to scan the entire area, look for the stimuli that would make your puppy react, and do a u-turn **BEFORE** the puppy gets above threshold.

Once you do a U-turn, I suggest you add another behavior, such as sitting or down, then reward the puppy for NOT reacting to the stimulus.

Watch Me Command

This command is taught to your puppy so that it will focus on you instead of something else. Remember that this will only work if they are below or at threshold. Practice in the green zone while the stimulus is at a low level of intensity, usually from a far distance.

Teach your puppy to sit and look at you by letting them smell a high-value food reward and holding it to your forehead, saying the command "watch me." When the puppy locks their eyes with yours, mark the behavior with a "yes," and give the food reward. The "watch me" command will get your puppy out of making bad decisions, provide mental stimulation, and teach an incompatible behavior to reactivity.

Troubleshooting

What happens when your puppy won't move?

This is very common for young puppies. You will need to have some high-value food reward such as chicken, hot dog, or cheese to lure them into starting moving. Once they begin moving, they should be fine. Keep the food on hand, just in case they get scared and decide to put on the brakes. Dixie did this for the first few weeks, and I always had some food with me to encourage her to keep moving.

How do you get the puppy to stay still to put the collar or harness on them?

Get the high-value food, training treats, or kibble out and drop some on the floor. Once they go to eat the food, put the collar or harness and leash on them and begin the training. This works every time for even the most hyper puppies.

You tried the loose leash walking technique yesterday, and it didn't work; what should you do?

This 6-step Loose Leash Walking process will take weeks or months to implement. This is done in multiple days. Only move on to the next step once your puppy has mastered the current stage. If your puppy is having trouble with one of the steps, move back to the previous step and practice that.

Your puppy wants to pick everything up off the ground

Teach the "leave it" and "watch me" commands. Redirect them to focus on you instead of the ground. Be consistent at reinforcing the puppy when they look at you. Another way to do this is to have some of their food by your side and near their nose so that they learn to keep their head up instead of

I have used the Starmark Pro Training Collar® (shown below) for giant dogs with small owners who can't handle their dogs on a walk. These breeds include Saint Bernards, Rottweilers, Doberman Pinschers, German Shepherds, and some Labrador and Golden Retrievers.

It would be best if you carefully used prong collars with little puppies. Slip leads work much better for dogs under 20 lbs. I briefly used the Starmark Pro Training Collar® with Dixie when she was about nine months old. However, I was very gentle with the corrections, and after about a month, she did not need it anymore, and we returned to a flat collar.

Equipment for Balanced Training:

- **Slip Lead** - This is a one-piece leash that slips over the head of the puppy and tightens around the top of its neck, just behind the ears. You will see these in many dog shelters, veterinarians, and groomers. My favorite slip leads are high-quality and made in the USA by Mendota Pet.

- **Prong collar** - These collars are used as part of a balanced training system by some dog trainers. They apply pressure on your puppy's neck and require your puppy to figure out how to release the pressure by doing what you want. This is not an ideal way to train a young puppy, so I recommend positive reinforcement. I use a Starmark Pro Training Collar®, shown in the photo below. It's made of hard plastic and less evasive than a metal prong collar.

What About Shock Collars?

A shock collar, also known as an E-collar or Remote Collar, can also be used in the balanced training method. You can vary the level of stimulation to achieve your desired result. You can also use a vibration or beep sound with most remote collars.

I am not an expert in shock collars. I have never used a shock collar. Therefore, I cannot provide additional details on effectively using them in this book. A popular book I recommend for this topic is *Everything You Need to Know About E Collar Training* by Larry Krohn.

Conclusion

You must implement the principles in this book and follow through with daily practice for it to be effective. This is for anything you want to master, not just leash training your puppy.

In addition to creating discipline, obedience, structure, and a routine for your puppy, nothing is more important than the consistency you implement into your puppy's life. Daily practice is essential. One lousy day walking your puppy, with them pulling and reacting, could set them way back in their training.

Don't underestimate the power of calm, confident leadership when handling your puppy on a leash. Your demeanor and your mindset will have a direct and lasting impact on your puppy's behavior.

Reread the chapter on Proper Mindset. This is the most critical part of the book. If you learn nothing else from this book besides this principle of proper mindset, it is well worth your investment.

A Final Note on Leash Training

Walking a puppy can be unsafe in some communities, which is why I always carry a bottle of Halt Dog Repellent Spray when walking Dixie. Made with capsaicin, an extract of peppers, that causes an intense but temporary sensation of heat and extreme discomfort to instantly subdue aggressive dogs. I would never leave home without a bottle of this attached to my belt buckle. It protects Dixie and me from stray dogs that could be aggressive.

Find Us Online

Book Website: puppytraining.dog

Visit our website for links to our social media pages Facebook, Instagram, and YouTube.

If you are interested in puppy training either in person in Huntsville, AL, or online, please visit Top Gun Dog Training's website at topgundogtraining.com

You can see these leash training drills and demonstrations on this YouTube channel: https://www.youtube.com/c/TopGunDogTraining; go to the playlist Leash Training.

Made in the USA
Coppell, TX
18 February 2023

13051372R00036